# WOMEN'S WORLD OF MONEY

A Life-Charging Beginner's Guide to Creating a Path for
Financial Independence, Success, and Closing the
Gender Bias Gap

OLOJO CHRISTIANA

# INTRODUCTION

Women's World of Money: A Life-Changing Guide to Creating a Path for Financial Independence, Success, and Closing the Gender Bias Gap is a new book that speaks of vital problems brought about by such very simple reasons on why men and women do not get rich as easily or establish their own businesses. Despite all the tremendous progress taken toward gender equality in the world, women still have more obstacles on their path to financial independence and success. In this book, I am going to shed lights on several issues that stand in the way of women's economic independence and give practical ways of closing the gap.

Equally, it seeks to give women some tools they need to be successful in their business and financial endeavors. Kindly journey with me and understand the systemic injustices that have kept women down for generations by looking at a lot of historical context, current data, and factors added to the wealth gap between men and women. By considering some of the reasons for these differences, we begin to appreciate how gender bias, pay inequality, limits in resource accessibility, and social norms raise the barriers women must climb if they are to amass wealth and launch their own businesses.

Reciprocally, I would want to design an action plan by detailing how one can become wealthy: financial knowledge, business avenues, and investment opportunities. We can enable women to take responsibility for their own financial futures and open new ways to prosperity by equipping them with all the knowledge, skills, and tools to handle this world of finance. I also would like to touch on issues of women in pursuit of financial independence, such as discrimination against them in finance, limited cash access, and problems of work-life balance. By being aware of and getting rid of such problems, we could be more supportive and provide a friendlier environment for women to become successful in their respective entrepreneurship and income-generating activities.

Most importantly, this book is intended to empower women in breaking down barriers, tearing down glass ceilings, and pioneering their own routes toward financial and business success with the ability to break through the barriers of a gender wealth gap. We want all women to thrive and prosper in a world that values and supports them economically Join us on this life-changing path.

# CONTENTS

Title Page

Copyright

TABLE OF CONTENT

INTRODUCTION

ACKNOWLEDGMENT

CHAPTER ONE: CLOSING THE GENDER WEALTH GAP
CHAPTER

TWO: THE POWER OF FINANCIAL LITERACY

CHAPTER THREE: BREAKING BARRIERS TO
ENTREPRENEURSHIP

CHAPTER FOUR: INVESTING IN YOUR FUTURE

CHAPTER FIVE: WOMEN AND CAREER TRANSITIONS

CHAPTER SIX: CULTIVATING LEADERSHIP SKILLS

# ACKNOWLEDGMENTS

I am eternally grateful and indebted, and I wish to thank all those who assisted in bringing out this book, "Women's Money: Women's Guide to Financial Empowerment and Bridging the Gender Gap."

Above all, I would love to extend my gratitude to my family, who tolerated me during those agonizing days when I had to write continuously. They have encouraged and inspired me, and for that, I am thankful.

I would also like to thank my friends and colleagues who provided helpful comments and recommendations which enriched the information contained in this book.

Lastly, I would like to thank my readers for their dedication in the development of women within the banking sector and taking time to go through this essential topic. Your commitment and support are highly appreciated.

We value that all of you are joining in to contribute to gender equality and financial development.

# CHAPTER 1
# CLOSING THE GENDER WEALTH GAP

I will be encouraging women to take charge of their finances and overcome institutional impediments to economic growth. I will also discuss the gender wealth gap, its causes and few of the many hurdles women face in generating and conserving wealth, from understanding disparity, Strategies for Wealth Building, Overcoming Barriers and Advocacy and Policy Recommendations.

## Understanding the Disparities

Through the book, I try to explain several causes that bring about the differential distribution of resources and wealth among these different groups. In fact, much is to be done in charting from where this historical economic disparity first originated, to further analyzing those structural impediments that continue to foster these gaps. This will allow the readers to understand more fully the pervasive nature of poverty in our world by highlighting the whole range of biases and exclusions that underlie these differences.

## Historical Context

The historical context of wealth accumulation based on gender differences is found in social norms and structures that have long favored men over women in monetary matters. Historical exclusions from resources, economic opportunities, and rights of inheritance have built a disparity in the accumulated wealth between men and women. It is this understanding of history that brings home the depth of inequality guiding women today in their earning capacity.

## Current Statistics

Although things are, indeed, getting better on the road to equality between genders, the latest statistics nonetheless paint a somewhat sobering picture where women are concerned with building up fortunes and attaining financial independence. There have been numerous studies indicating that women are less financially literate on average, receive less income than men, and are underrepresented in managerial and highly compensated jobs. All these inequalities add up to making women poorer than men; hence, this has dire implications for women in the accumulation and investment of wealth later on in their lives.

## Factors Contributing to the Gap

Various variables determine and explain the gender gap in accumulated wealth. These include discriminatory treatment against women in the workplace, unequal pay, limited access to capital and financial resources, and cultural expectations that reward men's economic success over women's. Once these variables are identified and wholly comprehended, it is possible to begin to address the causes lying beneath the wealth gap and to act toward leveling the playing field for women in the pursuit of finance and entrepreneurship.

# Strategies of Wealth Building

## Financial Literacy

The female gender should receive full financial education if ever the gap in financial wealth between men and women is to be reduced. Educate and equip women with knowledge and capability to take full responsibility for their financial security and long-term wealth creation through knowledge sharing, enabling them to make prudent financial decisions, manage active finance, and plan for a secure financial future. This provides them with the ability to take control of their financial destinies.

## Entrepreneurship Opportunities

The pursuit of entrepreneurship offers women one avenue to achieve economic independence and the building up of wealth. Empowerment of women through the creation and expansion of enterprise, generating income, and acquiring assets is possible by fostering opportunities for female entrepreneurs. This might be achieved by providing mentorship and training programs that help women entrepreneurs overcome wealth disparity between men and women, hence assisting in building a diverse and inclusive economy.

## Investment Options

Even though investment is one of the key avenues toward wealth accumulation, women are absent in most financial landscapes. By disseminating knowledge on investments and creating opportunities for women to invest, we can enable women to start building their wealth and securing their futures. For women, long-term financial security can be achieved by encouraging them to invest portions of their money in a variety of investment types such as stocks, bonds, real estate, and other assets.

# Overcoming Barriers

## Gender Bias in Finance

It is hard to believe that financial business, due to gender bias, is acting as a limitation to women's access to opportunities, resources, and support. Knowing and challenging the existing gender bias in the financial sector would enable the construction of a more inclusive and fair financial system, which would permit women to prosper. This will ensure that promotion of diversity and inclusion across all levels in financial institutions, leadership positions, and investment decisions is affected to remove obstacles and level the playing field for women at all levels in the financial sector.

## Access to Capital

One of the big hurdles standing between a few women and their desire to emerge on their own and set up businesses pertains to access to capital. We work to provide access to various forms of finance, like loans, grants, and venture capital, which are essential to enable women to start or expand businesses, invest in education, and build wealth over time. This can be realized through women-owned businesses and women-led initiatives on one side, supported based on putting high priority on gender-inclusive funding. The capital divide will shrink, and women will become empowered in reaching their financial goals.

## Work-Life Balance Challenges

One of the major issues for most women is how personal and professional demands can be balanced; this factor inherently influences their potential to pay attention to income generation and entrepreneurship. Offering women an opportunity to fulfill their financial aspirations, while maintaining their well-being and looking after their family responsibilities, involves the use of supportive policies and programs in work-life balance. Examples of these policies and programs that they may enact include but are not limited to flexible work arrangements, parental leave policies, and childcare subsidies. Establishing a work environment that is supportive-that is, recognizing and being considerate of the different kinds of needs out there-decreases the burden associated with challenges to do with work-life balance and creates space for them to flourish at work and in income

# Advocacy and Policy Recommendations

## Legislative Initiatives

Narrowing the wealth gap between men and women relies on advocating for legislative proposals that advance gender equality, female economic empowerment, and financial literacy. We can help create a more just society that values and promotes women's economic security by supporting policies to address pay equity, job discrimination, and access to financial resources. From the legislative point of view, one would logically argue in support of legislation that empowers the rights of women to level the playing field, hence enabling them to achieve financial success, furthers diversity, and guarantees equal opportunity.

## Business Initiatives on Inclusion and Diversity

This can also be achieved through inclusion and diversity business initiatives which will bridge the gap in the wealth of females and males, hence economically empowering the woman. The point is that allowing companies to focus on gender diversity in their recruitment procedures, leadership development initiatives, and workplace policies could further help women pursue successful careers and build wealth by giving them more access to resources that put them on the path to prosperity. As a matter of fact, we can create an inclusive and diverse workforce that benefits women and society in general. This would be achieved through the development in the organizations of a culture that is inclusive, fair, and supportive.

**Community Support Programs**

These community support programs are meant to assist in availing to the women all they require to engage in financial and entrepreneurial areas successfully which may be done through mentorship initiatives, networking clubs, and even financial literacy classes. By building strong support networks among women and fostering collaboration, we can enable them to overcome challenges, share knowledge and experiences, and access opportunities for development and improvement. Investing in community programs that put the empowerment of women first, and teaching women about finances, will create a more welcoming and encouraging atmosphere for women to flourish and reach their monetary objectives.

# CHAPTER 2
# THE POWER OF FINANCIAL LITERACY

Financial literacy is integral to economic development and gender equality. In this chapter, it will be shown how financial literacy can be one of the very powerful modes of women's empowerment in bringing wise decisions over creation of wealth and securing their financial future. In this way, readers will develop the skills and confidence they need to function in today's financial world. Knowledge and education can totally change women's relationships with money and point out new avenues to success. This chapter introduces the following topics: Importance of Financial Education, building a Strong Financial Foundation, Investing in Your Future, Financial Wellness and Well-being, and Empowering Others Through Financial Literacy.

## Significance of Financial Literacy

Financial literacy will, therefore, enable them to plan their financial futures and wipe off male-female disparities in affluence. Quite apparently, prudence in making financial decisions rests upon the four cornerstones of personal finance-budgeting, saving, investment, and debt management. The focus today is on financial education that thus prepares women with adequate knowledge and capability to deal with complexities in the world of finance and to achieve goals self-confidently and independently.


## Strategies for Budgeting and Saving

The cornerstones of one's financial foundation are mainly budgeting and saving. By creating a budget that details income and expenses and outlines savings goals, women can plan their expenditures, prioritize their needs based on financial importance, and work toward achieving financial security. Accompanying women in practicing the different money-saving tactics will enable them to create a financial cushion that would harm them and prepare them for the unforeseen financial problems that might befall them anytime in the future. These include setting aside a percentage of salary for contingencies, building up savings on a regular basis, and cutting out unnecessary expenses.


## Understanding Credit and Debt Management

One of the most important areas of financial literacy with implications for female financial well-being involves proper management of credit and debt. A proper understanding of how credit works, maintaining a good credit score, and responsible debt handling are all ways in which women can access affordable credit options, qualify for loans and mortgages, and avoid falling into financial pitfalls. By acquiring the necessary knowledge for judicious use of credit, debt repayment, and avoidance of high-interest loans, women will be able to improve their current financial health and establish a strong foundation for the future.

## Setting Financial Goals

Setting monetary objectives will powerfully motivate women to take responsibility for their financial situation and strive to achieve their goals. On determination of both short and long-term financial goals, a route is shown to women for their financial journey, and this keeps their eyes fixed on their goals. Examples of such goals include having savings for a house, starting a business, or reaching a stage where one would retire nicely upon reaching retirement age. Setting SMART objectives-that is, specific, measurable, attainable, relevant, and time-bound-will significantly help women track their progress, make adjustments where needed, and celebrate reaching milestones in finances over time.

# Investing for Your Future

## Introduction to Investing

Investment is one of the important tools for gaining wealth and achieving financial independence. It is important that women learn how the basics of investing in stocks, bonds, mutual funds, and retirement accounts can help them, with time, gain wealth and achieve their major long-term financial goals. A woman who makes investment decisions based on a general understanding of the proper ways to invest, who identifies her risk tolerance level and then diversifies her portfolio, is said to be congruent with her financial goals and values.

## Types Investment

There are many different types of financial opportunities available to women; each has attendant risks and returns that may be realized. The investment opportunities available to women run the gamut from low-risk-such as savings accounts and certificates of deposit-to higher-risk investments such as stocks and real estate. These opportunities can be offered to them, depending on their financial goals and risk tolerance. The good portfolio will, therefore, be created by women investing in a range of asset classes and industries, which will bear ups and downs in the market economy. In that way, it will protect

9

them against risk and multiply the returns, further fortifying their portfolios.


### Risk Management

Investment strategy will also be greatly determined through risk management. After determining the risk tolerance, investment goals, and diversifying their assets between different asset types, women will be better positioned to limit their exposures to risks, protect themselves against the volatility of the market, among other unforeseen events. Ability to face the challenge of investing's complexity successfully, and to make decisions that are in tune with their financial goals calls for women to comprehend the risk-return trade-off; do homework well in advance of investment decisions and seek advice whenever necessary.


# Financial Wellness and Well-being

### Mental Health and Financial Stress

The stress that comes from financial situations may bear heavily upon women's mental health and general well-being. Managing financial stress, worry, and concerns about money is important in maintaining mental well-being and developing resilience to financial setbacks. Being in control of these things is key to managing one's money. It will enable them to take care of their mental health and well-being and tackle their financial fears in a positive and constructive manner through self-care, reaching out to loved ones for help, and coming up with healthy ways of coping.


### Building Resilience and Coping Strategies

In case of financial reversals, resilience is required in putting one on his feet so as to direct his way through unexpected financial eventualities. Women may be able to wait out financial adversities resiliently and may rise with determination from a set-back by coping methods. A few examples of such tactics are emergency fund creation, seeking financial guidance, and looking for alternative sources of income. It can help them develop an optimistic view towards life, openness to change, and learning from past experiences-all indicators of achieving resilience, which can allow women to not only survive under arduous financial conditions but emerge stronger, more confident, and empowered. These are all things that can help women create resilience.

**Seeking Professional Help**

Seeking professional assistance from financial advisors, counselors, or psychotherapists is another means through which women can seek help to sort out complicated financial problems, make fully informed decisions, and thereby enhance their financial welfare. Women can get the most important resources, skills, and techniques needed to manage their personal finances themselves, reduce stress, and achieve financial stability by going to the right professionals specializing in finance, mental health, and personal wellbeing. When women take that step and decide to seek professional help, they are making the stride necessary to take control and empower themselves with decisions that will lead them toward total happiness.

# Empowerment of Others: How to Create Financial Literacy

### Teaching Financial Literacy in Schools

Financial literacy should be taught at a very young age to empower the next generation, especially the young woman, for knowledgeable decisions about her finances in building a financially secure future. Rather, teaching girls' financial literacy in schools, basic money management skills, and inculcating financial awareness at tender ages will give them knowledge and confidence when approaching the challenges of adulthood, both successfully and in reaching their financial goals. It is here that the goals will be achieved.

## Community Workshops and Programs

Financial literacy seminars and programs within the community will help women gain more knowledge and acquire better financial skills. Such workshops and programs are very important, as they equip women with useful tools, support, and opportunities for networking. In seminars that would cover topics such as budgeting, investments, debt management, and financial planning, women can get the detailed knowledge from professionals, network with other women, and be in a position to access various tools and resources that will empower them to take control of their finances and, in due course, build wealth. Therefore, investment in community programs that may be educative in instilling financial literacy will eventually pave the way for a more supportive and receptive atmosphere in building up the desire in women for financial independence and success.

## Mentorship and Support Networks

Availability of mentorship and support mechanisms is important in ensuring that women realize their aspirations regarding financial independence and entrepreneurship. Connections among women with mentors, role models, and support networks can be arranged and facilitated to encourage, advise, and provide women with opportunities to develop and grow in the fields of finance and business. Good mentorship relations, support groups, and networking with people of similar values and visions will help women through the problems, overcome various obstacles with confidence, and resiliently accomplish all kinds of financial and entrepreneurial goals.

# CHAPTER 3
# BREAKING BARRIERS TO
# ENTREPRENEURSHIP

Breaking Barriers to Business dives deep into the unique venture capital and entrepreneurship challenges and opportunities of women. It covers systemic barriers and biases standing between women and business success-from the landscape of entrepreneurship through overcoming fear and self-doubt, getting support and mentorship, overcoming obstacles as a woman entrepreneur, celebrating success, and paying it forward.

Women need to come out from traditional stereotypes of gender roles, discover their economic potential, and avail opportunities opened for them in the fast world of running a company. This chapter emboldens, educates, and advocates for women in defining success on their own terms and shapes a more inclusive and diverse corporate world for future generations.

# The Entrepreneurial Landscape

The environment of entrepreneurship offers a unique opportunity to women in follow-through of passion, creation of new solutions, and successful firm building that can contribute to the economic growth and impact on society. It is only when women feel confident with at least a basic understanding of the mechanics of the ecosystem surrounding entrepreneurs, successfully identify market opportunities, and develop their talent pool and expertise to advantageously position themselves for the challenge that they can effectively face challenges and possibilities linked to entrepreneurship. The reason being the backdrop of entrepreneurship is never immobile; it allows women to show their capabilities-to be an agent of change and a force for good in influencing society through their business.

## Overcoming Fear and Self-Doubt

### Building Confidence and Resilience

It is important that women develop self-confidence and resilience to become fearless and confident in pursuit of their entrepreneurial dreams with determination and perseverance. Women should nurture a growth mindset, attainable objectives, and celebration of every small accomplishment done, which will surely allow growth in self-confidence and motivation and not be irresolute about problems. In establishing a support structure made up of mentors, peers, and allies, women will also be capable of overcoming self-doubt and acquiring sufficient confidence to flourish as entrepreneurs. That would give them the confidence to be encouraged, receive feedback, and support from those people.

### Embracing Failure as an Opportunity to Learn

Perhaps one of the biggest mindset changes will be embracing failure as an opportunity to learn, which will help women overcome their fear of failure and take calculated risks toward their entrepreneurial journey. It is when failure is seen as a steppingstone toward success, lessons are drawn from missteps, and plans are altered based on feedback and insight that such women get developed emotionally and professionally, build resilience, and achieve their entrepreneurial goals with confidence and drive. This would be because if women learn to view failure as just part of the process and not some sort of taboo to be avoided at all costs, they would not fear decisions, trying new things, and growing in their businesses.

### Seeking Mentorship and Guidance

Mentors and guidance provide a source from which women entrepreneurs may draw much-needed knowledge, advice, and support to overcome a host of obstacles to entrepreneurship by accelerating the growth of business enterprises. This could be achieved through mentors and guidance sought. They would be kept in close contact with the mentors who share values, goals, and a vision to make sure women are privileged in an enormous variety of knowledge, resources, and opportunities to learn, grow, and succeed in their entrepreneurship venture. The good mentorship relationships, seeking constant feedback, and learning from the experiences of others will significantly empower these women against self-doubt in decision-making based on facts; hence, they will realize their full potential as an entrepreneur.

# Access to Resources and Support

### Funding Options for Startups

Access to cash is an important issue that can make a critical difference between the success or failure of a startup business. There is gender discrimination and institutional obstacles within the financial industry that may impede the ability of female entrepreneurs to access cash, loans, and investors. These are challenges that women entrepreneurs encounter unlike their male counterparts. By investigating alternative funding possibilities-m Crowdsourcing, angel investors, venture capital, and government subsidies, for example-female entrepreneurs can master the financial challenges of financing their business ideas and confidently scale up their companies in a resilient way. Besides, women can try to increase their possibilities of successfully establishing and scaling their firms by building a strong financial strategy, constructing a compelling business case, and networking with potential investors. This encompasses all forms of assistance that will help women achieve the required capital.

## Networking and Relationship-Building

She should know how to network and build relationships in order to grow a business and expand professional connections. These sets of skills would facilitate entry into resources, opportunities, and support systems. Events, networking groups, associations, etc., about other entrepreneurs with interests related to one's business can help women build better contacts, partnerships, and collaborations that may open up new areas for prospects, clients, and marketplaces. In addition, social media, online platforms, and digital technologies can also serve in building their networks, demonstrating their capabilities, and reaching out to potential customers, investors, and other business associates in building their journey as entrepreneurs.

## Harnessing Technology for Growth

Technology can act as a strategic driver to develop entrepreneurs by streamlining the operations of the businesses and scaling up the enterprises. Indeed, digital technologies, e-commerce platforms, and online marketing methodologies have helped them expand the visibility of their services, attract more clients, and grow their businesses in the highly competitive markets. Investment in technology, automation, and acquisition of digital skills therefore helps them organize the operations of the company better and further enhance their productivity while staying ahead on the power-surfing curve of the fast-growing digital economy. By using technological advancements for growth, women entrepreneurs can have their business stand out, adapt to new situations, and capitalize on the new opportunties that arise in order to be successful in the world of entrepreneurship.

# Overcoming Obstacles: Woman Entrepreneur

## Gender Bias in the Business World

Women entrepreneurs also have to face the all-pervasive gender bias in the business world, affecting not only their level of access to capital and opportunities but recognition for success. It may enable difficult preconceptions, breaking down barriers and creating a level playing field, and supports women entrepreneurs to succeed through the promotion of gender equality, raising awareness about gender prejudice, and supporting initiatives that promote diversity and inclusion in entrepreneurship. In contrast, a strong support network may be built through mentorship and giving voice to women in business that can enable women to negotiate gender bias, overcome hurdles, and achieve success on their own terms.

## Balance Work and Personal Life

Many estimates say that women entrepreneurs face pervasive gender discrimination in the business world; such discrimination influences not only access to finance and opportunities but also the recognition of success. It may eliminate preconceived notions, break down boundaries, and even level the playing field. It thus calls for the success of women entrepreneurs through attainment of gender equality, creation of awareness on gender discrimination, and support for projects facilitating diversity and inclusion in entrepreneurship. However, this can be flipped into a strong support structure in terms of mentorship and giving women a voice in business. For example, women can learn how to work their way around the bias, break through the barriers, and emerge on top their own way.

### Overcoming Imposter Syndrome

Imposter syndrome is yet another psychological barrier more than gender bias that may wreck the confidence of women, the belief in themselves, and their sense of being immersed in entrepreneurship. In fact, recognizing imposter syndrome, reframing negative self-talk to positive affirmation, and praising achievement and ability are strategies through which women can transcend the feeling of self-doubt to feel self-confident, acceptant, and even proud of their unique talents and contributions as entrepreneurs. By seeking help from mentors, peers, and mental health professionals; by showing self-compassion and taking responsibility when it is time to move past limiting beliefs, women can get over imposter syndrome, step into their power, and pursue entrepreneurial aspirations with honesty and resilience. These are all ways that women can help themselves.

# Celebrating Success and Paying It Forward

### Identifying Achievements and Milestones

One of the most important ways women can acknowledge their achievements, take stock of where they have been, and continue to remain energized on their path as entrepreneurs is to recognize achievements and milestones. By setting goals for themselves, monitoring their achievements, and celebrating the passing of important milestones they reach along the way, women will build momentum, build self-confidence, and stay focused on their long-term vision of success. It is the celebration of triumphs-no matter how small those successes might seem-which keeps women pushing boundaries, taking chances, and reaching their fullest potential as entrepreneurs.

### Supporting Other Women in Business

One of the strong ways of giving back to the community, sharing experiences, and building a support network that fosters collaboration, development, and enabling is by offering support to other women in business. This includes women facilitating the creation of a more inclusive and diverse entrepreneurial climate that fosters and promotes the valuable economic and social contributions of women. This would also be achieved through the mentoring of budding entrepreneurs, showing resource and support networks towards women-led enterprises. By fostering a support culture, collaboration, and empowerment for women in business, that ripple of positive change in inspiration and success ripples back to all members within the entrepreneurial community.

## Giving Back to the Community

Providing assistance to fellow women entrepreneurs is a strong way of giving back to them for their experiences and building an enabling network that encourages cooperation, growth, and empowerment. Women can enable a more representative and diverse entrepreneurial platform that values and enables the contributions of women to economic life and society as a whole. This may be achieved through the mentorship of young entrepreneurs, sharing of resources, and even giving support to enterprises headed by women. Creating a culture of support, collaboration, and empowerment among women in business has the potential to generate a domino effect of positive change, inspiration, and success that is beneficial to all members of the community of entrepreneurs.

# CHAPTER 4
# INVESTING IN YOUR FUTURE

Women investors are unique because of specific problems they face, such as the gender pay gap, a greater lifespan, and lower risk tolerance. That is why we help them by offering personalized solutions to their issues.

We also focus on financial literacy and goal setting, plus long-term strategic planning, to build an investment portfolio that will see out market ups and downs while consistently returning income. This chapter helps women take responsibility for intelligent investment decisions and grow their money intentionally by championing financial literacy and the empowerment of women.

## The Magic of Compound Interest

Due to this fact, women should, therefore, know the magic of compound interest in order to start amassing wealth and becoming financially independent. In view of the fact that women were able to invest early enough, with persistence and proper planning, then full optimization of the power of compounding on savings and passive income would be wholly optimized for long-term investment gains. This, in turn, will enable them to accelerate the process of building wealth by snowballing and catapult them toward financial success and stability in the long term with the aid of compound interest earned.In other words, income will not only be made on an initial investment, but it will also be made on interest earned. There are various advantages that compound interest coupled with sensible investment choices accrue to women in establishing a better financial future, attaining their objectives, and building a more secure future for themselves and their children.

# Building a Diversified Investment Portfolio

### Stocks, Bonds, and Mutual Funds

Consequently, women, through a well-diversified investing portfolio, can control the risk and earn higher returns on their investments toward the realization of goals. Therefore, she would be able to generate a very strong investment portfolio that would act as a cushion during the time of market volatility or economic slowdown, provided she apportions her investments across different asset classes, such as equity, bonds, and mutual funds. They could therefore spread the risk and thereby be in a better position to exploit market opportunities, and hence construct a portfolio which would be resilient against market ebbs. Mutual funds allow for diversification and professional management, while equities give the potential for growth. In turn, all of these features give women a chance to conduct their investments in such a way as to allow conformity with their level of risk tolerance, time horizon, and financial goals. Growth is achieved through stocks, income and stability through bonds, and diversification through mutual funds. Through diversification, it is the case that the women can thereby acquire a balanced portfolio, make the returns less volatile, and, in turn, improve their long-term investment performance through diversification across different asset classes.

## Real Estate and Alternative Investment

Other means through which women can diversify their financial portfolio and create passive streams of income and wealth are in unconventional asset classes. An investment in real estate properties will provide a woman with a regular stream of rental income, probably an increase in capital value, and protection from inflation. Properties in this category include commercial real estate, rental property, and investments in real estate investment trusts. The diversification into private equity, hedge funds, and commodities can further help women investors improve their overall risk-adjusted returns. These vehicles offer the woman investor unparalleled investment opportunities, uncorrelated returns, and potentially high yields. Further investments by women in real estate and alternative investments would extend the horizon of investment to new paths of growth and provide a diversified portfolio that would fit with their overall financial goals and their risk tolerance.

## Retirement Planning Strategies

One of the major concerns that occupies significant prominence with regard to investments for the future is retirement planning. This is because it will ascertain that the female has a happy, secure retirement style without hurting their financial stability. Women can build up their nest egg, save more money for retirement, and create a secure financial future in retirement through designing a retirement plan, establishing savings goals, and investing in available retirement accounts like 401(k), IRA, and annuities. This will, therefore, enable the women to maximize their retirement savings, minimize taxation, and confidently and securely achieve retirement goals with methods that ensure efficiency in taxation, maximize employer contributions, and diversify retirement investments. Women have placed retirement planning at the top of their list to take control of their financial futures and plan a worthwhile retirement so that when they reach their golden years, they will be able to enjoy the fruits of their effort.

# Risk Management and Asset Protection

## Insurance Planning

Long-term investment should therefore incorporate retirement planning. It will ensure women retire comfortably and in security without personal financial constraints. Building a nest egg, increasing the amount of money saved for retirement, and investing in retirement accounts like 401(k), IRAs, and annuities will ensure that finances are secured for themselves in retirement. Instead, with tax-efficient methods for maximizing employer contributions and diversification of retirement investments, women can achieve maximum retirement savings with minimum tax burdens while executing their retirement goals in complete confidence. By prioritizing retirement planning, a woman takes charge of her own financial future and plans a retirement that will be rewarding, enjoying fruits from the effort put in during the golden years.

## Estate Planning

Estate planning is the process resorted to in order to legally protect the assets and transfer them onto heirs. This will also enable women to safeguard their legacies, optimize tax liability, and ensure that their property is transferred in a manner in which they may desire. An appropriate estate plan can include a will, trust, power of attorney, and health care directive to enable women to plan for the day when they will no longer be capable of taking care of themselves or their loved ones. Consulting professionals in the estate planning arena, such as attorneys, financial consultants, and tax experts, might not only help women sort through the intricacies of estate planning, but also serve their own needs and wishes for their particular and unique goals, hence creating a personalized plan that truly reflects what they believe in and stand for. Estate planning is considered one of the proactive strategies for women to protect their hard-earned wealth, secure legacies, and provide for successive generations without stress and with peace of mind. There are a few advantages that come along with the estate plan.

### Tax-efficient investing

This is a tax-efficient way of investing that aims at minimizing the taxes of women and maximizing their after-tax profits with the assurance of maximum after-tax growth. Expertise in the tax laws, the tax-advantaged accounts, and efficient techniques in investments of taxes will help the women reduce taxes while accelerating growth or hanging onto investment gains. Utilizing Iraqi individual retirement accounts, 401(k) plans, and 529 plans allows women to delay taxes on investment gains and reduce their tax liability today, all while allowing money to compound. Tax-loss harvesting can help, as does capital gains management and diversification among taxable and tax-advantaged accounts toward better optimization of tax efficiency and improved after-tax returns in the pursuit of financial goals more efficaciously.

# Socially Responsible Investing

### Environmental, Social, and Governance Criteria

While an ever-increasing number of investment decisions meet the ESG criteria, one associated emerging trend involves socially responsible investing, popularly known as SRI.

It, in turn, enables women to invest in those organizations that consider vital social responsibility, corporate ethics, and sustainability. She can opt for those companies that put a strong focus on care for the environment, social impact, and corporate governance by having ESG criteria embedded within the investment research process. Therefore, women investors can create competitive financial returns in addition to contributing to the environment in a positive way. Some of the key ways to connect values to investment decisions include women investors who invest in ESG funds, green bonds, and impact investments that would bring good change to the world and contribute to making a more sustainable and equitable future for society and earth. Such are the funds through which women can align their values with their choice of investment. Socially responsible investment provides ways to make a difference with one's investment dollars in causes important to them and a positive influence through the decisions made in investments.

## Impact Investing

Impact investing is one concept of socially responsible investment. It seeks to create good social and environmental impact in concert with financial reward. This form of investment allows them to contribute to projects, companies, and funds that deal in sustainable development and fosters relevant social issues. These investments into impact funds, social enterprises, and community development projects let one fund programs related to gender equality, education, healthcare, and conservation of the environment, with a correlated financial return on investment. Impact investing enables women to connect their financial goals to their values, thus creating real changes for good in the world by using their investment capital. This would be something they could call their own. Impact investing would, therefore, be a way to give them an opportunity to commit resources. influence, and experience in ensuring an inclusive, sustainable, and thriving future for all.

## Alignment of Value with Investment Decision

The very foundational idea of socially responsible investment is that of value alignment with investment decisions. This approach offers the possibility of investing in those businesses and initiatives that represent a woman's values, beliefs, and goals. If women can undertake due diligence to investigate the environmental, social, and governance practices of companies, as well as assess the impact such practices have upon society and the environment, they can make intelligent investment choices more in line with their values, furthering positive change in the world. Through business investing that fosters diversity, sustainability, and social responsibility, women can support causes that matter most to them, create impact in their communities, and build an ethical and sustainable financial portfolio. By integrating principles into the process of investment decision-making, women will be able to invest in their objectives, have marked impacts on the world with their money, and create a better future for themselves and their forthcoming generations.

# Financial Independence and Freedom

### Setting Financial Goals and Milestones

Alignment of Values with Choice of Investment: The very concept of socially responsible investment involves investments in a manner that values get aligned with decisions. This may provide them with the ability to invest in businesses and programs that align with their personal values, beliefs, and objectives. Where women undertake due diligence, investigate environmental, social, and governance practices of companies, and evaluate what kind of an impact such practices have on society and the environment, they make informed investment decisions that better align with their values and contribute to positive change in the world. Through business investments that further diversify, sustain, and show social responsibility, women support causes they care about, create impact in their communities, and build a better, more ethical, sustainable portfolio of investments. A merging of values with investment decisions means women are investing with purpose and making an impact with their money to secure a better future for themselves and the next generation.

### Achieving Financial Security

Women need to aim at financial security in order to protect themselves, their family, and their future against the uncertainties of the financial world. The establishment of an emergency fund, debt management, and maintenance of a diversified portfolio will afford women greater insulation against sudden setbacks and long-term financial security. The application of a risk management method will help the woman protect her assets and mitigate risks through methods such as insurance planning, estate planning, and tax-efficient investing to protect the financial future from sudden disasters. Financial security enables each woman to approach life's challenges with confidence, peace of mind, and to know that any financial hurdle can be overcome and success achieved in any setting.

## Enjoying the Fruits of Your Labor

The ultimate reward for women who have put in a lot of effort, made sound choices regarding their finances, and accomplished their financial goals and aspirations is the time to enjoy the fruits of their labor. Self-care, wellbeing, and work-life balance are just some of the things women should really afford themselves-to enjoy the moments of success, celebrate achievements, and actually take pleasure in this road to financial freedom and independence. They can begin to focus their appreciation on the opportunities and experiences that are afforded to them as a result of achieving financial independence through resting, recharging, and indulging in activities that bring them joy and fulfillment. This will indeed help women realize the worth of their hard work and give them time for reflection with appreciation for life. The action of enjoying the fruits of your labor now reminds women to celebrate successes, embrace accomplishments, and live life confidently with purpose and in a thankful manner.

# CHAPTER 5
# WOMEN AND CAREER
# TRANSITIONS

This chapter will take the women through the dynamic career landscape so as to make informed choices, overcome some challenges, and seize the opportunities for growth and advancement.

Changing careers, job market success, and new career beginnings pose challenges and create opportunities that are also explored.

## Assessing Your Skills and Interests

Quite logically, assessing one's skills and interests should be an important first step in the process of negotiating job transitions for women. In undertaking a self-assessment-that is, assessing one's talents, limitations, passions, and values-women may clarify their objectives regarding work aspirations and avenues for growth and development. The clearer women are about their skills and interests, the more effectively they can link options of work with their personal and professional goals; thus, making active choices about the career path they get on, and pursuing opportunities that resonate with their talents and passions. This is where identification of their potential and interests enables women to capitalize on their distinctive talents, investigates new opportunities, and initiates them on a career path that will not only be meaningful and rewarding but also identified with their personal identity and fulfillment of goals.

# Exploring Different Career Paths

## Networking and Informational Interviews

The women who would like to explore other career paths, extend their professional network, and get an inside view of what is happening within various industries, jobs, and possibilities can thrive with informational interviews and networking with other professionals. It provides a chance for women, through networking-contacts in the field, attending networking events, and also contacting mentors and industry experts-to gain practical information, advice, and guidance regarding possible career options, prerequisites required for each specific job, and emergent trends in the industry.

Through the process of engaging in informative interviews, women may learn about the experiences of others, build relationships, and come across hidden opportunities. Such opportunities might create new prospects for one's career, possibilities of cooperation, and possibilities of growth. Informational interviews and networking opportunities are two of the significant tool's women should have to be able to negotiate successfully in transitions in their careers and widen their horizons to make informed decisions about their professional development and growth.

## Professional Development and Skill Building

With the increasing investment in professional development and enhancement of skills, thereby being able to meet the changing market requirements for career growth within the constantly changing work world, women will be enabled to be competitive. Opportunities given for continuous learning-workshops, courses, certification, and seminars-in lieu of earning them-will enable women to acquire new skills, learn the business, and make more career choices for themselves. With transferable skills in communication, leadership, problem-solving, and digital literacy, women will have successful career transitions, pivot to new jobs, and thrive in a rapidly shifting labor market. Professional development with skill building will finally give them the grounds on which they can pursue their professional goals and aspirations with confidence and competence. This then puts women in a position where they can remain relevant, flexible, and relentless in their working.

**Considering Entrepreneurship and Freelancing**

Entrepreneurship and Freelancing: This also would allow for added flexibility, autonomy, and control in their professional lives, giving them the ability to follow their hobbies, create their own businesses, and build other sources of income. Further, allowing the exploration of entrepreneurship and freelancing as career options can give women such added benefits. It gives a wide opportunity to women for tapping into their creativity, innovativeness, and spirit of entrepreneurship by considering either entrepreneurship, side hustle, or freelancing in their line of expertise. This gives them an avenue for diversifying their revenue streams and opening up more avenues toward growth and success. It means that turning into entrepreneurs or freelancers, women open themselves to being their bosses, masters of schedule, and working on initiatives that fit their values, interests, and goals. They can take responsibility in their professional future through self-employment and freelancing by creating a relevant portfolio that is satisfying according to their unique talents and objectives.

# Dealing with Job Loss and Finding a New Job

## Coping with Job Loss and Uncertainty

This is about being resolute, able to adapt easily, and optimistic while going through the job loss process and managing one's career change, which may be a painful emotional experience for women. They could lose their jobs, manage uncertainty, and negotiate the emotional rollercoaster often associated with career transitions with grace and resilience as they acknowledge their feelings, are assisted by friends, family, or professional counselors, and therefore practice self-care and self-compassion. With the growth mindset, optimism, and looking at job loss as an opportunity for personal and professional growth, women can reframe their point of view, be more resilient, and arise even stronger from setbacks and problems occurring along the way in their career. These are all things that can benefit women.


## Updating Your Resume and LinkedIn Profile

This means women need to constantly update their LinkedIn profiles and resumes so as to brand themselves appropriately for a new professional opportunity and job transition that recognizes capability, experience, and accomplishment. They can catch the attention of recruiters, hiring managers, and future employers by building an attractive CV, mentioning major achievements, and tuning their profile to some position and fields. This will definitely make them stand out in the highly competitive job market. All they need to do to heighten their visibility and credibility for professional pursuits is to fill out a LinkedIn profile, create a quality professional network, and connect to their peers and industry thought leaders. Manage Job Loss; Move into New Role; Position for Success in Your Career Journey An updated resume and LinkedIn profile will prove to be strategic should one lose their job.


## Interview Preparation and Job Search Strategies

In this respect, referring to the paragraph above, one of the most significant competencies during a career transition negotiation in the pursuit of new opportunities offering better professional development and growth would be interview preparation and elaboration of effective job search strategies. With a little study about businesses and interview questions, and with an effective showcase of one's abilities and expertise, it is quite easy for women to ace the job interviews, make the best impression ever, prove their value to the employer, and thus enhance their chances of getting the job they want. By developing a job search plan, using online job boards, attending events to network, joining professional associations, and through referrals and recommendations, women will be able to uncover their hidden job opportunities, extend their professional networks, and lubricate the wheels of job searches. Hence, with preparation on interviews and methods for job search, women can confidently, professionally, and strategically negotiate career changes. This helps give clarity and drive to career objectives and desires of women.

# Negotiating Job Offers and Advancing Your Career

### Approaches Toward Negotiating Salary

An important skill that women need in their quest for careers and in their struggle to get paid equally is the art of negotiating jobs offered and striving to get what is due as salary. Researching the going rate for their field, learning what their current market value is, and stating their worth and value allows women to negotiate pay, benefits, and perks commensurate with their talents, experience, and knowledge. With improved bargaining, training in the practice of assertiveness, and career coaching by the mentors or career coaches at each and every step in their careers, women would be better prepared to negotiate pay and speak up for themselves in order to get favorable terms in the form of job offers or promotions. Salary negotiation techniques give women the tools to fight for pay equity, negotiate their value, and grow their professions confident and financially empowered.

### Mentorship and Career Counseling

It is one practical means whereby women receive support,

guidance, and sympathy in the form of accessible seasoned professionals serving as mentors and role models who help by sharing experiences and views relevant to career choice problems and opportunities. These should be desirable to obtain by finding mentors and career counseling. Matching women with mentors, having a relationship established, and drawing feedback and recommendations relevant to career goals and aspirations could help women receive practical wisdom in ways to grow their network and accelerate professional growth and development. A mentor will be able to help the individual to realize how to overcome certain challenges, seize opportunities, and be all they can be through guidance on career transitions, skill building, networking opportunities, and leadership development. It is a step-in career journeys for a woman to seek mentorship and career guidance. This could be a very good avenue for the people to seek support, guidance, and inspiration from the teachers in overcoming such barriers and realizing their full potential in growing their professions with confidence and clarity.

## The Establishment of a Career Development Plan

Another strategic tool for women is the construction of a career development plan that allows them to set objectives and outline a career path with a view to plan and implement professional growth and success in a structured and systematic way. By setting career goals, critical milestones of reaching those goals, and concrete steps to take towards those goals, it becomes possible for women to roadmap their path to success-that is, to monitor progress and stay focused and motivated toward their goals. An individual's career development strategy can be developed through the assessment of his talents, making both short-term and long-term goals, and then seeking advice and mentorship in them; it also encompasses commitment to continuous learning and development relevant to one's industry. Creation of a career development plan helps women to take responsibility for their own professional development, to focus their efforts toward meeting their goals, and negotiate career transitions with direction, clarity, and certainty. In this way, women will become what they are capable of and prosper in their chosen career track.

# Work-life Balance and Wellbeing

### Encouraging Self-Care and Mental Health

In relation to work-life balance and how to manage stress for a sustainable career, women need to be empowered on how to take care of themselves and their mental wellbeing. Those women who will invest in themselves by devoting time to exercise, meditation, mindfulness, and hobbies will reduce symptoms related to burnout, increase resilience, and boost well-being even more. Such activities give women a rejuvenating opportunity to refresh their bodies, minds, and spirits. They can have a healthy and sustainable work-life balance by seeking mental health specialists, counselors, or support groups that enable them to set boundaries effectively, delegate duties, and manage the workload. Women who exercise self-care and mental health are likely to love their jobs and live resilient lives, hence contributing to their well-being and success.

### Setting Boundaries and Managing Stress

There should be a proper balance between work and personal life, managing stress, preservation of wellbeing and effectiveness at work. Exercising, meditating, paying attention to their activities, and engaging in hobbies reduce burnout and increase resilience to better the general wellness of women. These are activities that help women stay physically, emotionally, and mentally fit. This balance, as far as professional responsibilities and personal life are concerned, can be effectively managed by the women themselves with the help of mental health specialists, counselors, or support groups and also by setting boundaries, reassigning responsibilities, and managing the workload in such a manner that can help attain a healthy and workable balance between work and life. A woman who takes priority in self-care and mental health would be far better equipped for performance at work, maintaining resilience, and creating a meaningful and balanced life that supports overall well-being and success.

**Enjoy Your Profession**

The other key goal for women is to find their calling, passion, and happiness in their work. In that way, they will get significance and delight from the job done and be satisfied. That is significant because getting satisfaction from your profession is a number one objective for women. Furthermore, it enables women to link the workplace to values and interests, hence having strength so as to do meaningful work, make a positive difference, find fulfillment, and have a purpose in daily activities and achievements.

The career growth of women, therefore, becomes purposeful, rewarding, and significant in their journey when they involve themselves in challenging and inspiring projects that provide them with opportunities for growth and learning apart from contributing to a cause that is important to them. Women who find their careers meaningful are able to develop sentiments pertaining to satisfaction and contentment that go beyond career achievement and a paycheck. This would also prepare the woman for future growth and excellence, enabling her to make some difference in her field of activity.

# CHAPTER 6
# CULTIVATING LEADERSHIP SKILLS

For a woman to become a successful manager both in work life and beyond, she has to learn certain skills and strategies, challenges and opportunities presented.

The chapters cover issues such as understanding your leadership style, effective communication and relationship building, decision-making and problem-solving, motivating and inspiring others and leading during change and challenge.

## Understanding Your Leadership Style

A basic step in positive leadership competencies development among women is to understand your leadership style. It would not be impossible for a woman to perceive her own leading style, strengths, and areas where improvement is needed through reflection on values, communication preferences, and strong points. Knowing whether they are more transformational, democratic, or servant in style empowers a woman to correct her approach to leadership in light of her values, goals, and business culture. In so doing, she can be herself as a leader and inspire other people toward pertinent change. Better recognition of a woman's personality, values, and what she stands for thus allows her to lead with confidence and authenticity, producing better results through her leadership style. This will allow her to maximize her strengths, flex her leadership style, and develop a style uniquely her own.

# Effective Communication and Relationship Building

### Active Listening and Empathy

To the extent that one is concerned with the development of good communication skills, gaining trust, and building a solid relationship with team members, colleagues, and stakeholders, women are encouraged to practice active listening and show empathy. By listening to others carefully, trying to perceive the other person's point of view, and showing empathy and compassion, women can create a helpful and friendly work environment. This would create an environment where team members will have an opportunity to feel heard, appreciated, and treated as human beings. Empathy through active listening will help foster a culture that values open communication, trust, and mutual understanding; women can build rapport, settle issues, and work effectively through proper communication with others. By engaging in active listening and empathic listening practices, women will contribute to the improvement of their communication, foster their relationships, and exercise leadership characterized by empathy, compassion, and honesty. As a result, a friendly and encouraging work environment will be in place to enable their team to blossom and achieve many successes.

## Giving and Receiving Feedback

It is a very important skill to develop in women-a knack for giving and receiving feedback. This would enable them to guide, support, and develop their team members, and on the other hand, allow them to seek feedback for themselves to improve their performance and leadership effectiveness. Women can involve their team members in growing, learning, and blossoming in their jobs by giving feedback in a positive way, focusing on behaviors and outcomes, and providing suggestions for change that are specific and actionable. Development in women would thus be heightened: self-awareness, effective communication skills, and leadership effectiveness created through feedback being given openly and honestly, advice is sought from others, and reflection on areas they might need to improve. This will afford the ability to adapt, learn, and move forward as leaders. Women who can give and receive feedback-that is a two-way process for growth, development, and continual improvement-can perform the act of leadership with openness and transparency in the achievement of excellence.

## Conflict Resolution and Mediation

Probably one of the most important leadership skills a woman can have in her portfolio is the one which can effectively handle and mediate conflicts and disagreements to create collaboration, iron out differences, and sustain a cordial work atmosphere. Women can diffuse tensions and build consensus among team members through solving problems in advance, listening to all sides, and seeking common ground and mutually beneficial solutions. Mediating disagreements in a nonjudgmental manner, facilitating free-flowing discourse, and encouraging constructive communication may resolve problems for women, strengthen relationships, and create a work culture that is healthy and inclusive, valuing diversity, equity, and respect for all. Moreover, the conflict resolution and mediation skills within the women themselves, while negotiating problems, will build cohesive teams and drive success together in their businesses. These gifts further equip women to command with diplomacy, tact, and emotional intelligence.

# Decision-Making and Problem-Solving

### Strategic Thinking and Planning

Capacity-building of women in leadership on strategic thinking and planning will help them make valid-information-based decisions, set well-defined goals, and deal effectively with complex problems and opportunities. Data analysis, trends, and market dynamics allow women to tell in advance the definition of what future trends and strategic priorities are linked to business objectives. Strategy is an enabling tool that allows women to think critically, prioritize the initiatives, and come up with sound decisions that bring about long-term success and sustainable growth for their businesses. This is because through strategic thinking, women can think strategically. It empowers them to develop skills in strategic planning, setting SMART goals, and evaluation to unleash their potential to lead a team or organization with vision, purpose, and strategic clarity toward successful and innovative outcomes.

### Analysis of Risks and Opportunities

Among the most important elements of good decision-making and problem-solving for the women running management positions is the art of making out risks and opportunities. In this regard, risk assessments, scenario planning, and SWOT analyses allow women to have in sight dangers, problems, or opportunities that influence the performance and success of their business ventures. Through the identification and analysis of risks and opportunities, women can make informed decisions to reduce likely dangers and seize new trends and opportunities that come their way. This therefore strengthens the capacity of their businesses in terms of creativity, agility, and resilience. As their capabilities to manage risks develop, also the harnessing of stakeholder input and consideration of alternative scenarios, women can lead with certainty, with vision and strategy. The businesswomen will then know how to manage volatility, make the most of the opportunities and ensure further growth and prosperity for the companies they serve.

### Making Ethical and Responsible Choices

Women follow a very essential leadership principle: to make ethical and responsible decisions. It means that women can make ethical decisions based on social responsibility and organizational principles in order to foster an environment of integrity, transparency, and accountability inside their enterprises. This is achieved by giving due consideration to ethical implications, values, and stakeholder interest.

The women must demonstrate ethical leadership through acts of moral courage brought forward by setting priority on ethical concerns, seeking out diverse viewpoints, and then acting in ways which are honest, fair, and respectful to others. For them to be able to make these ethical decisions, they are supposed to foster in themselves the development of trust, credibility, and reputation as an ethical leader through decision-making that is ethical and responsible. This may in turn be further inspiring to the others to uphold ethical norms, values, and principles in their professional behavior and decision-making.

# Empowering and Motivating Others

### Delegating Tasks and Building Trust

To empower people, create autonomy, and drive performance and engagement within teams, women need to be capable of effective delegation and building trust with other members of their team. It forms one of the most important leadership competencies. By delegating responsibilities based on the distributed talents, abilities, and development goals of the members in their team, women effectively delegate duties to their team, build trust, and empower the team for work ownership for the success of the business.

The building of trust via open communication, transparency, and accountability helps women establish a culture of high performance and collaboration within the teams. It is a culture in which all members of the team are made to feel appreciated, supported, and motivated to turn in unsurpassed performances in their jobs. They can achieve collective objectives, drive innovation, and develop a culture of mutual trust, cooperation, and excellence in their teams by unlocking the potentials, skills, and abilities of the team members through a proper delegation process entailing building trust.


**Recognizing and Rewarding Success**

Recognition and rewarding achievement is one of the strong leadership practices that women leaders should hold in high regard. This practice helps women inspire, motivate, and retain top talent within their organizations. This would also help foster an appreciative culture of recognition and celebration of successes. By recognizing efforts, milestones, and successes of their team members, women are capable of boosting morale, reinforcing positive behaviors, and creating a culture of recognition and gratitude that empowers and involves their team members. This would also include incentives for them, bonuses, promotions, or public acknowledgement of their performances.

The retention of the best performers themselves drives performance and ingeniously builds a culture of excellence and achievement in their respective teams. Also, when women are recognised and acknowledged for their achievements, this serves to allow them to inspire, motivate, and retain top talent. This leads to a culture of appreciation, recognition, and excellence that, in turn, fosters corporate success and employee engagement.

### Fostering a Positive and Inclusive Work Environment

Since it is an imperative strategy to create a culture of diversity, equity, and inclusion by appreciating and embracing unique insights, experiences, and perspectives that each member possesses, women should ensure the work environment created or fostered is positive and inclusive. Women have the ability to foster a healthy, inclusive work environment, wherein opportunities are allowed to prosper for all members of the team, to contribute, and be successful.

This can be developed with programs for diversity, equity, and inclusion, open communication, and opportunities to collaborate and belong. Such women would serve as examples to other people, support the implementation of diversity and inclusion initiatives, and help build a respectful, empathetic, and welcoming culture where difference is embraced-a culture of community spirit instilling a sense of belonging within their teams-ultimately, for the sake of fostering a positive work environment. It is necessary to consider that women can create a culture of inclusion, respect, and teamwork in the workplace by creating an enabling environment. This form of culture ensures innovation, engagement, and also leads to corporate success.

# Leading Through Change and Adversity

### Embracing Innovation and Adaptability

Amidst a high-paced, ever-changing corporate environment of change, uncertainty, and disruption, embracing creativity and adaptation is one leadership talent for women to respond aptly to such times of evolution. They can empower their teams to be creative, agile, and resilient by fostering an enabling culture of invention, experimentation, and continuous learning. This can enable them to adapt their teams in ever-shifting markets and technological leaps-to the wants of customers. If harnessed, innovation and adaptation would build confidence and resilience in driving opportunities and navigating around problems. Equipped with this, women can lead with agility, inventiveness, and foresight. This latter condition corresponds with leading the team and organization through change, uncertainty, and hardship with an openness to innovation and flexibility. Such predisposition actively assists the woman leader in developing a culture of creativity-agility-resilience as a drive toward sustained growth and success.

## Resilience in the Face of Challenges

Of the many leadership competencies important for women, perhaps one of the most crucial relates to developing resilience in response to adversity. It is through this process that setbacks, failures, and obstacles may be overcome with grace, persistence, and perseverance. These same adversities, failures to learn from, and coming out of adversities even stronger are possible if women develop emotional intelligence, learn about themselves, and the art of coping. Women who possess resilience hold their concentration, optimism, and proactiveness intact during adversity.

This, in turn, will empower them to lead with confidence, flexibility, and courage even in situations that are exceptionally challenging. In developing resilience in the face of adversity, women are granted the powers of surmounting obstacles, using setbacks as lessons, and leading others with perseverance and determination, even with elegance. This hence mobilizes them to be able to endure, learn from, and grow through adversities themselves and for others.

## Inspiring Others to Overcome Obstacles

An inspirational practice of transformational leadership by women leaders involves motivating, empowering, and supporting their team members in solving challenges, setbacks, and uncertainties with courage, resiliency, and determination. This can be achieved by inspiring others to remove obstacles. By relating and sharing personal experiences of fighting challenges, setting examples, and extending support, encouragement, and guidance, women become capable of persuading their fellow team members to triumph over challenges, learn much from failures, and grow resilient and powerful enough to face

43

more problems. It is expected that the women business leaders themselves project leading with empathy, authenticity, and vulnerability to inspire others to get over barriers. It is achieved by creating a safe and supportive environment where team members are empowered, motivated, and driven to address their challenges and seize opportunities the very moment they present themselves. Women can build a culture of resilience, courage, and growth within teams by inspiring others to break down barriers. This enables women to negotiate challenges, embrace change, and accomplish success with confidence, drive, and grace.

# CHAPTER 7
# EMBRACING DIVERSITY AND
# INCLUSION

The aim of this chapter is to discuss how business and ethics support diversity and inclusion. The business case for diversity and inclusion is informed by the sense of inclusion of a diverse workforce, better recruitment and retention, fairness and equity in the workplace, and the involvement of different stakeholders.

## Business Case for Diversity and Inclusion

By reading the business case for inclusion and diversity, women in leadership positions will better understand the importance and benefits and effectiveness of fostering a diverse and inclusive workplace. Precisely, diverse teams realize greater success in solving challenges more imaginatively and more creatively, which results in more effective decision making, heightened productivity, and better financial performance. On one hand, embracing diversity and inclusion opens a wide pool of talent where women leaders can hire the best personnel for their respective organizations, and innovation and success develop within those hired. Embracing diversity and inclusion improves the organization in employee engagement, morale, and the retention rate. This leads to establishing a very healthy work culture where all employees are valued, shown respect, and are free to provide their unique perspectives and skills. It becomes a business issue because women leaders drive business performance, create cultures of inclusion and diversity, and attain that competitive advantage that enables their companies to be successful and sustainable well into the future. This can only be a reality if they are steeped in the business case for diversity and inclusion.

# Creating a Culture of Belonging

### Diversity Training and Education

Awareness, cultural competency, an inclusive and belonging culture are some of the important elements a woman leader should try to instill within her businesses through programs on diversity training and education. It means that the women leaders could train employees, managers, and leaders in the need for diversity and inclusion through training in topics like unconscious bias, cultural awareness, and inclusive leadership.

This training may provide them with knowledge and competencies needed to be fostered in creating a workplace that is both fair and inclusive. Diversity and education training help women leaders fight against prejudices, stereotypes, and impediments to inclusion. This also allows leaders to create a truly inclusive culture where everybody feels valued, respected, and supported for being themselves at work. The cultures of belonging and inclusivity, where diversity is celebrated, as well as where all employees grow and prosper, can be created by women leaders through investment in training and education on diversity. It allows them to create knowledge, understanding, and empathy among their employees.

### Employee Resource Groups and Affinity Networks

The best avenue toward giving a sense of community, support, and belonging to people of various origins, identities, and experiences will be through the creation of employee resource groups and affinity networks. By constituting groups on similar identities, hobbies, or experiences, the leaders will be able to give a platform for connecting, networking, and supporting one another. The organization would, therefore, feel a lot more connected, more comradely, and inclusive.

Employee resource groups and affinity networks could be used to highlight the varied perspectives, opinions, and successes of the female leaders. That would create an enabling and more inclusive workplace where all employees feel valued and respected and can bring their whole self to work. The culture of valuing and embracing all employees in their uniqueness and lived experiences may be further shaped by women executives. It would involve leading or actively supporting affinity networks or employee resource groups in implementing activities that advance an organization's inclusion and diversity awareness or build a sense of belonging.

## Addressing Implicit Bias and Microaggression

How unconscious bias and microaggression are dealt with forms the base upon which one can create an inclusive culture for the women leaders in development by making a safe, respectful, and fair workplace for both employers and employees. The women leaders would thereby be able to lead their colleagues in realizing the importance of getting over biases, stereotypes, and microaggressions.

This would in turn make a workplace more attractive and friendly to all employees. While combating unconscious prejudice and microaggression, women leaders need to provide the staff with training, resources, and support that would help them recognize and work out their own biases. Valuing diversity in people from all walks of life is important for the women leaders in building a culture. Identifying unconscious prejudice and microaggressions helps the woman leader build a culture of inclusion, respect, and equality. It is the kind of culture that needs to make each employee feel valued and respected, allowing them to bring unique experiences and talents into the workplace.

# Recruiting and Retaining a Diverse Workforce

## Implementing Inclusive Hiring Practices

Women leaders should apply inclusive hiring policies in the attraction, recruitment, and retention of a diverse pool of talents that reflects the diversity of their client base and community. If adopting inclusive recruitment strategies, women leaders are able to attract a diverse pool of candidates and select based on skills, qualifications, and potential rather than biases or stereotypes.

Inclusive strategies that would be included in their example list include diverse interview panels, removing bias from wording within job descriptions, and blind resume screening. Inclusive hiring practices of women leaders may lead to the creation of a diverse and skilled workforce, the sparking of creativity, and a culture that fosters inclusion and belonging around diversity by embracing equity at work. The application of inclusive hiring practices, no matter where they are applied by the woman leader, allows organizations to recruit top talent, further enhance organizational performance, and establish a culture that values diversity, fostering a setting for all workers to thrive and succeed.

## Mentorship and Sponsorship Programs

Mentorship and sponsorship programs are, in practice, policies which women executives can enact to help better professional development, career advancement, and retention among diverse talent at their companies. Matching employees with mentors and sponsors who will be engaged to help guide, encourage, and advocate for them will help women leaders facilitate employee career trajectories while eradicating many of the obstacles in the way of opportunities for growth and development. Accordingly, women in leadership are allowed to develop pipelines of diverse talent, help further diversify leadership, and establish a culture of support, empowerment, and inclusion that values the potential of all employees and fosters their development. Mentorship and sponsorship should be institutionalized by women in leadership in a way that plants the culture of mentorship, support, and advancement into their organization. This enables the environment in which diverse talent would thrive, succeed, and confidently lead with authority in their organizations.

## Advancing Diversity in Leadership Positions

There is a strategic imperative for the women in leadership positions to ensure that diversity in the leadership positions advances to full representation, equity, and inclusion throughout all levels of their respective organizations. Women leaders can foster a culture that values and furthers diverse representation of leadership, perspectives, and experiences by establishing diversity goals, tracking the progress made toward achieving those goals, and holding the leadership accountable to provide forward motion on diversity and inclusion.

This would involve women leaders identifying and developing diverse talents, giving them opportunities in leadership development, and creating pathways to leadership positions or promotion opportunities for underrepresented groups. Women leaders can use diversity in leadership positions to build a culture of inclusion, equity, and representation. This culture gives diverse leaders the right environment to foster innovation, collaboration, and organizational success; it creates an inclusive workplace that is more equitable for all employees.

# Promoting Equity and Fairness in the Workplace

## Pay Equity and Transparency

To help ensure justice, equity, and inclusion in their organization's pay schemes, pay equity and transparency is something all women leaders should enact as an integral practice. The women in managerial positions are in a position to inspire a culture of equity, fairness, and trust by performing routine pay equity audits, by taking action to handle pay disparities, and by espousing transparency in the way compensation is performed. This culture will appreciate and reward employees for their skills, contributions, and performances rather than on the basis of biased or discriminatory reasons.

The promotion of pay equity and transparency will facilitate the empowerment of women executives to fight against gender and racial pay inequity, fairness, and equity in the compensation system, and build such a culture that will honor and respect the contributions of all employees. Pay equity and pay transparency can make it so that women in positions of authority create a culture of equity, trust, and inclusion. In these kinds of cultures, all workers are assured that they will receive pay equitably for their work and have equal opportunities for growth, progress, and success across the organization.

## Flexible Working and Work-Life Balance

Women leaders will support flexible working arrangements and work-life balance to build an organizational culture that is respectful of employees' well-being, health, and personal or family life. This is important for women leaders to be able to meet the various needs, preferences, and responsibilities of employees. The leaders can thus help the employees strike a balance in their responsibilities at both the professional and personal levels by offering flexible work arrangements, such as working from home in a flexible hour or compressed workweek schedule.

The workplace would be enabling and inclusive, recognizing and valuing the different needs and priorities of all employees. In this case, women leaders enhance the talent pool in the firms, employee satisfaction, and perceptions of employee well-being and health by creating a work culture that supports work-life integration. They promote flexible working and a balance of life and work, hence bringing forth a culture of flexibility, well-being, and inclusivity. This culture shall help each employee to succeed and be at their best, realizing full potential at work and in personal life.

### Support the Well-being and Mental Health of Employees

It is by creating a culture of caring, supportive, resilient organizations that genuinely care, and place health and wellness at the forefront, support their employees in their well-being and mental health. A culture for women leaders can be provided with resources, wellness programs, and support services that relate to mental health, create well-being, resilience, and self-care. It would be a culture where the aftercare of one's mental and emotional health would be encouraged, and one would seek help and support if they so choose.

In essence, this is where leaders in particular realize that the feelings and wellbeing are psychological; they would understand that they were in a safe and supportive environment that genuinely values and supports holistic wellbeing for all its staff. It fosters a culture of empathy, compassion, and care, resilience, engagement, and better performance. The leaders could create a well-being, care, and support culture that values and prioritizes health and happiness, empowers growth and success, and offers the best to the organization-that is, support for employees' mental health and well-being.

# Engaging with Diverse Stakeholders

### Building Relationships with Customers and Communities

In order for women leaders to build relationships with customers and communities for understanding, engaging, and serving different client groups, there is an organizational need and strategic imperatives to produce products, services, and experiences that meet particular requirements, preferences, and expectations of these consumer groups.

By interacting with diverse consumers, seeking their input, and listening to their opinions, women leaders can gain insight and build trust that leads to loyalty and advocacy across a variety of consumer segments. This leads ultimately to gains in customer satisfaction, retention, and loyalty. This means that women leaders can actually bring about an enabling culture, one that will place the customer in the middle, innovate, adapt dynamically according to the condition of the changing market, and more importantly, accelerate growth and success for institutions through their relationships with consumers and communities. Ladies leaders can thus foster customer-centricity, culture, empathy, and creativity that genuinely considers and gives preference to needs and preferences across various customer groups through the process of relationship-building with customers and communities that drives customer happiness, loyalty, and advocacy.

## Partnering with Diverse Suppliers and Vendors

Here, partnering with diverse suppliers and vendors is a strategic step on the part of the woman leader to move forward with diversities, equity, and inclusion within her supply chain and at the same time build economic opportunities for various businesses and entrepreneurs. As such, women leaders will be able to develop a more inclusive supply chain through the procurement of goods and services from a diverse range of suppliers, advancement of minority-owned businesses, and support for various initiatives on supplier diversity that empower and value diversity among suppliers and vendors.

In this way, by working with a diverse base of suppliers and vendors, the women leaders can help create economic empowerment, opportunities for underprivileged entrepreneurs, and an enabling culture of inclusion beyond the enterprise to the supply chain and the overall ecosystem. Collaboration with a diverse base of suppliers or vendors would allow women leaders a better opportunity to enhance supplier diversity, foster economic empowerment, and generate social impact. It replaced the more diversified and balanced value chain that enabled different enterprises and entrepreneurs to spur economic growth and wealth creation in their communities.

## Contributing to Social Impact and Corporate Responsibility

Contributions at the strategic level by these women executives toward corporate responsibility for social impact should result in good change and ensure social value which would enhance communities and societies. Women leaders can act in the interest of solving social and environmental challenges through inner alignment of values, mission, and resources for social impact. Community development will ensure and promote sustainable responsible business for the interest of the people and the environment.

Accountability anchored in social and environmental dimensions can, therefore, allow women leaders to exercise social impact and corporate responsibility that will create a culture of purpose, impact, and sustainability and elicit positive change within and beyond their communities. In light of social impact and corporate responsibility, women leaders can have a highly valued and influential role in creating value in the development of positive change that benefits organizations, communities, and the global landscape. This is a gift to the legacy of impact, purpose, and sustainability, thus encouraging others to lead with intention, empathy, and accountability.

# CHAPTER 8
# SUSTAINING SUCCESS AND LEGACY

In this concluding chapter, I will discuss important strategies and psychological shifts that are necessary to take place if a person is to lock in a financial legacy and contribute meaningfully into the next generation. Long-term financial goals are set and personal development investments are made. The chapter touches on building a support network, navigating life transitions, giving back to the community, and leaving a lasting legacy. Empower the woman with an understanding and wherewithal to take responsibility for their own economic futures, to rise above challenges, and become role models in encouraging future generations in their pursuit of financial independence and self-determination.

## Defining Your Personal and Professional Legacy

### Reflections

Impact and Values-Making a Contribution Looking back on your impact and values involves reflecting on what you believe in and what you would like to contribute to the world. This is a precursor to defining your professional and personal legacy. An accounting of core values, strengths, and passions provides the woman leader an opportunity to define purpose, vision, and mission-create decisions and actions in concert with values and goals. Success can be defined, through values and impact, by women leaders themselves by reflecting on them, setting goals for themselves, and thus leaving behind legacies reflective of their values and beliefs apart from the contributions they have made to organizations, communities, and society. It is through reflecting back on values and impact that women leaders can develop in themselves self-awareness, authenticity, integrity, and a legacy congruent with their values, passions, and aspirations. This in turn will enable others to lead with purpose, passion, and to make an impact.

## Setting Long-Run Goals and Aspirations

These are long-term objectives and aspirations which women leaders need to build a route map for their success and professional and personal development. The setting of clear, specific, and attainable goals makes women leaders focused in concentrating their energies, resources, and efforts on what is most important to them.

They can imagine, make a long-term dream of the future that perhaps motivates and enables them to act and pursue their aspirations. Long-term goals and aspirations set by women leaders will enable them to more vividly dream of an ideal future, overcome many obstacles and barriers, maintain focus and commitment for the realization of their desired outcome, and leave behind a legacy. Accomplished women leaders will define long-term goals and aspirations that will make their legacy typify values, passions, and aspirations. By doing so, they will have inspired others to dream big, take calculated risks, and pursue goals with courage and tenacity.

## Building a Legacy Plan for the Future

One conscious step women leaders can make in the desire to deliver constant influence and lasting legacy, personally and professionally, is to develop a written legacy plan that describes their vision, greatest values, and future direction. A legacy plan helps women leaders specify their vision, mission, and values, and itemize the activities, resources, and support that would help them achieve their goals for improving their companies, communities, and society. In developing a legacy plan, each woman leader will have the chance to ensure that her decisions and actions are congruent with her values, goals, and desired impact.

They can also identify priorities, track the emergence, and assess success. The legacy plan-the road to success, growth, and influence-will be helpful in helping women leaders inspire others to lead with purpose, vision, and with impact. They also leave a legacy that symbolizes their values, passions, and achievements.

# Building Resilience and Continuous Growth

### Embracing Lifelong Learning and Development

The woman leader should embrace lifelong learning and development as she builds her resilience in realizing continued growth and commit to continuous personal and professional development. As a woman leader is open to new information, experiences, and skills, the capacity for adapting with change while remaining relevant and competitive will be built in an ever-changing business environment.

Embracing lifelong learning and development can heighten creativity, inventiveness, and leadership potential for women leaders and create success opportunities in business and career. Through lifelong learning and development, women leaders will build resilience, flexibility, and agility to embrace obstacles and uncertainties with confidence, curiosity, and a growth mindset. In doing so, they will be able to succeed and lead with influence and effect.

### Adapting to Change and Uncertainty

The ability to adapt to change and uncertainty in a rapidly

changing and turbulent world of business is undeniably one of the key talents that a woman leader should possess. It deals with barriers, derailers, and disruptions. Resilience, flexibility, and adaptability may, therefore, be developed by women leaders. They should take change, uncertainty, and ambiguity on board with confidence, creativity, and agility in responding effectively to unforeseen events or circumstances. Women leaders need to be flexible, receptive, and proactive in adjusting to uncertainty and change.

They must also welcome new experiences, challenges, and opportunities that will help them grow both as individuals and as leaders. By learning to accept change and uncertainty, women leaders are able to influence others to accept it, take calculated risks, and pursue development and transformation. They can also build resilience, courage, and confidence by leading with resilience, innovation, and impact amidst adversity and uncertainty.

## Overcoming Setbacks and Challenges

Overcoming setbacks and problems is important to allow women leaders to face challenges, failures, and setbacks and come out even stronger and resilient than before. This represents an important constituent process in the development of resilience and the fostering of continuous growth.

Through viewing setbacks and challenges as opportunities for learning, growth, and development, women leaders can engender a growth mindset in themselves, perseverance, and persistence that formulates the basis on which adversities are transformed into opportunities that will further growth, innovation, and transformation. Positive thinking, resilience, and being focused on the goals of the women leaders are what the women need to be successful in conquering the difficulties and challenges. Besides that, seeking help, feedback, and guidance will definitely help in overcoming the setbacks, hurdles, courageously, tenaciously and with determination.

Obstacles and challenges could be the experiences from where the women leaders may develop resilience, grit and tenacity. In that regard, they come out stronger, wiser, and with greater resolve to aspire for something very meaningful to make a difference that will endure through the lives and time of others with a good example and legacy that inspires others not to give up but to fight, innovate, and succeed against all odds and challenges.

# Mentoring and Paying It Forward

### Sharing Knowledge and Experience with Others

At this stage, the idea of mentoring and paying it forward comes in, in which an individual may share his knowledge, experience, and wisdom with others for development, growth, success, and even creating a culture of mentoring, learning, and empowerment in firms and society. Women in leadership may serve as mentors who provide a sense of direction, encouragement, and guidance toward the leaders. They may even guide these people to balance their career paths with struggling through difficult challenges that would help them achieve their goals with more confidence and resilience.

Shared expertise and experiences from the woman leader empower and inspire the future generation of leaders. Additionally, they would leave a trail of mentorship, support, and influence on growth, learning, and development in the organizations and society at large. Women leaders have the potential to foster mentorship, learning, and empowering cultures by letting others around them take advantage of their experiences and expertise. This culture was supportive and valued the growth and success of all people to allow a person to be part of the community, collectively giving support, enabling each other through collaboration to empower the people to thrive, be successful, and make a difference in an organization and society as a whole.

### Support the Leaders of Tomorrow

For them, investment in development, growth, and success in building the pipeline of emerging leaders and diverse talent representative of the leadership pool that the future will bring is a strategic practice-for their companies and communities alike. This can be done through the many supports being provided to the next line of leaders. They can develop talent, promote diversity, and create a succession planning leadership culture by affording aspiring leader's opportunities, resources, and support that will ensure continuity, creativity, and sustainability within their organizations and communities.

This would facilitate the growth of the next generation of leaders in their development, realization of their objectives, and confidently leading with impact and purpose within their communities and organizations. She will, therefore, be able to leave a legacy of influence, leadership, and mentorship from which other future leaders can draw. The enhancement of the culture of leadership development, diversity, and inclusion will, therefore, be fostered through valuing the potential and talent that all people possess, creating a community of collaboration, support, and connection that allows the women leaders to grow, be successful, and make a positive difference both in their respective organizations and society through support for the next generation.

## Investing in Mentorship and Coaching Relationships

It is better that the women leaders make it a point to invest in relationships with mentors and coaches, which would help them in their overall growth and development as a person and a professional. To this end, guidance, feedback, and support from experienced mentors and coaches are sought. By so doing, creating opportunities for mentoring and coaching relationships will better place women in leadership to gain insight, knowledge, and wisdom from others. Furthermore, leaders might still get support, encouragement, and accountability in achieving the set goals, pressing through obstacles, and reaching full potential as individuals and leaders.

These are the ways women leaders invest in networks, connections, and support systems to enable and nurture personal and professional growth. Further, they will leave a legacy of influence, support, and mentorship that will drive learning and development in businesses and society as a whole. It is also important that women leaders promote growth, development, and success through well-invested mentorship and coaching relationships. This can also enable them to establish a culture of learning and growth that allows every individual to value and support personal and professional development. This enabling culture, through a range of achievements, supports women leaders in contributing to their companies and society at large, builds realized potential, and growth.


# Integrating Purpose, Well-being, and Success

### Finding Meaning and Fulfillment in Your Work

The woman leader should focus on building up the mentorship and coaching relationship because this would pay off in business and personal life. For this, guidance, critique, and support from experienced coaches and mentors will be sought. In fact, the prospect of mentoring and coaching relationships for them will more suitably position the women leaders to learn from others.

The leaders might also be able to find the accountability, support, and encouragement they need in order to reach their goals, overcome setbacks, and realize their fullest potential as leaders and human beings. These mentoring and coaching relationships serve to enable and inspire growth, learning, and evolution both as leaders and human beings. The women leaders can leave a legacy of influence, mentoring, and supporting that foster learning, development, and growth in communities and organizations. It is also important that women leaders promote growth, development, and success through well-invested mentorship and coaching relationships. This can also enable them to establish a culture of learning and growth that allows every individual to value and support personal and professional development. In an enabling culture, women leaders can enable their organizations and society to thrive through their achievements.

## Prioritizing Health and Wellness

Taking care of oneself to maintain one's vitality and resilience as a leader and person is important. The process balances success, purpose, and well-being. Thus, women leaders are entitled to self-care, rest, and relaxation to retain a life-work balance and for better health and happiness. Such an approach may allow the women leaders to recharge, revitalize, and refill energy and attention. Health and wellness are the priority areas when the women leaders can maintain their vitality, resilience, and performance.

They will create strategies to navigate adversities, pitfalls, and uncertainties with poise, clarity, and resilience, that will enable them to be productive, effective, and powerful leaders to inspire and bring change. By being able to care for their health and wellbeing, women leaders can work with others towards a culture of self-care, balance, and well-being. It is the culture that facilitates every individual to flourish and achieve holistic well-being, building up a sense of resiliency, vitality, and fulfillment that predisposes them toward flourishing, succeeding, and impacting their organizations and society positively.

## Cultivating a Sense of Purpose and Contribution

Women leaders must establish a sense of purpose and contribution. They must align their actions and decisions with their beliefs, passions, and goals to create a meaningful and happy life and career. This is the only way that such a balance between success, purpose, and well-being will ever exist. By connecting to their innermost beliefs, passions, and desires, women business leaders can generate a sense of purpose, meaning, and contribution that not only orients their actions, decisions, and priorities but also drives them to make a difference in their companies, communities, and society at large.

It is through the installation of a sense of purpose and contribution that the legacy of influence, meaning, and fulfillment is reflective of beliefs, ambitions, and goals that women leaders can leave behind. This will further inspire others to lead usefully, with passion, and to make a difference in personal and professional life. The possibility of creating a life and career which is full of meaning, fulfillment, and in congruence with values, passions, and aspirations is open to women in leadership positions. This may give an impetus to others in pursuit of their goals to create positive legacies that reflect values, passions, and the contributions which they make to their organizations and society. This can be done by cultivating a sense of purpose and contribution.

## Leaving a Lasting Impact and Creating a Positive Legacy

### Making a Difference in Your Community and Beyond

Creating impact on the community and world at large in general means bringing about positive social and environmental change through diverse ways, such as applying resources, competencies, and influence to benefit the greater good of all. It is definite that with a legacy of influence, purpose, and contribution to society and the world, women leaders can amply contribute to the betterment and prosperity of their community. These can be achieved through involvement in social impact initiatives, volunteering, and donating toward charitable causes. A woman leader might use her potential impact within and outside her community to leave a legacy that is true to her values, interests, and even talents. This, in turn, would bring more inspired and motivated people to lead responsibly, humanely, and with the purpose of making their communities and societies better.

### Sustainability and Social Responsibility

Continue to create a legacy whereby businesses and communities can apply ways to achieve sustainability and social responsibility through social justice, economic prosperity, and the well-being of all stakeholders. It would also mean that women leaders could help instill a culture of accountability, transparency, and responsibility in business and society, while valuing and supporting people and the environment in addition to profit by bringing in sustainability and corporate social responsibility into their business model. This will also enable them to create a positive impact and to leave a lasting legacy that goes beyond the bottom line.

## Celebrating Achievements and Acknowledging Contributions

You should extend the ideas of sustainability and corporate social responsibility through your business and community and embrace practices that support a vision of environmental stewardship, social equity, and economic prosperity for all stakeholders in creating impacts that leave a lasting legacy. Leaders can create a culture of responsibility, accountability, and transparency in service of sustainability and social responsibility for the business operations, engrain values for people, the planet, and profit, and actually extend more positive change and impact within organizations and communities. Besides allowing women leaders to imprint their positive values, interests, and contributions, sustainability and corporate social responsibility ensure that others can lead with integrity, purpose, and responsibility too in a manner conducive to a more sustainable, egalitarian, and prosperous future for all.

# CONCLUSION

All in all, " Women's World of Money: A Life-Changing Guide to Creating a Path for Financial Independence, Success, and Closing the Gender Bias Gap" is an impactful and needed resource for women who want control over their financial futures and learn how to overcome those obstacles that stand in the way of equal wealth between men and women. In this book, we have discussed specific issues regarding personal finance that women face. From income disparities to social expectations and cultural norms about personal money.

I am equipping my readers with the understanding and skills to competently and confidently navigate their financial lives. Such topics as budgeting, investing, entrepreneurship, and negotiating means that best suit women are touched upon. Thus, they empower them to break loose from traditional gender roles and boundaries set by society for them and encourage striving to achieve financial independence and success on their own terms.

More than that, this book does not only provide the readers with real steps and at the same time practical advice on how to get financial freedom but also makes those subscribed to it feel all united and under protection. My book motivates and strengthens confidence in one's own potential and talent by sharing the experiences of real women who have triumphed over financial adversities and reached their goals.

The bottom line is that "Women's World of Money" is not just a beginner's guidebook, but a manifesto for change, an appeal to take action against the status quo by all women worldwide-to take matters into their hands where financial security is concerned and to head toward a more equal and inclusive future. This is a book that eradicates the gap in wealth between men and women and makes a way for women to take responsibility for their economic well-being, opening up a pathway to a more successful and equitable society for all.

It is when the financial empowerment of women is not only a want but a necessity that "Women's World of Money" stands out as a beacon of hope, a pathway to a better tomorrow. I hope its message touches the heart of each reader it gets to, in turn making my readers take responsibility for the power they have over their financial lives and rewriting this story for future generations.

# ABOUT THE AUTHOR

Olojo Christiana was the brain behind ' Women's World of Money: A Life-Changing Guide to Creating a Path for Financial Independence, Success, and Closing the Gender Bias Gap; She is an accomplished financial expert committed to empowering women worldwide.

Through years of work in the finance business, Christiana has come to a profound appreciation of the hurdle's women struggle to overcome for financial independence and to close the wealth gap between men and women. With the incisive writing and prudent advice provided, Christiana has managed to become a source of hope for women in reordering their financial destinies. 'Women's World of Money' remains a testimony to his interest in gender equality and financial development and should, therefore, be a must-read for women across all ages and classes.

www.ingramcontent.com/pod-product-compliance
Lightning Source LLC
Chambersburg PA
CBHW070125230526
45472CB00004B/1424